Cognac Kisses

DIANA WILLIAMS-KIRKLIN

I write the stories that bruise, heal, and stay with you.

Diana Williams-Kirklin

Cognac Kisses
ISBN: 978-1-968115-50-0

Published by Phoenyx House, an imprint of JMarie & Co. Publishing
Cover design and interior layout by Tirado Designs Printed in the United States of America

This is a work of poetry. Unless otherwise indicated, all pieces are original creations of the author. Any resemblance to real persons, living or dead, is purely coincidental.

For permissions, inquiries, or bulk orders, please contact: JMarie & Co. Publishing support@jmariepublishing.com

First Edition
Paperback Edition

For anyone standing in the doorway of a new beginning.
Refusing to shrink.
Standing after the fire.
Those redefining desire and want.
For those becoming.
For those who have discovered that chapter two energy.
Don't apologize.
Burn And Rise.

PLAYLIST

Cognac Kisses by Eden's Flame

Pink Toes & Pretty Dresses
Real Me 2
The Strong One
Watch Me Drown
Chapter 2 – Where I Begin
Playing Hard to Get
Loved By His Storms
Wicked Smile
My Exhale
Slow Burn
Hey You!
I Belong to Me
The First Time
I Burn
Long Days
Burn
Cigar Nights

SMOKE

"Pink Toes and Talons"

They know me as soft,
polite hands folded in my lap,
the kind who speaks with grace,
pink toes and pretty dresses,
eyes lowered just enough to seem demure.
Heaven-sent, they whisper.

But inside these pages
I loosen the leash.
A beast—beautiful yet free—
smoke on my tongue,
talons ready to shred.
The real me waits in ink and shadow.

They think they're ready
for candlelight and kindness,
but she is no dinner companion.
She's blood-warm, electric,
a current that scorches
anyone who wanders too close.

I keep her here for a reason.
You are not equipped—
you're a baby gazelle
with your throat exposed.
Come closer and she'll
leave you wrecked,
contacting your next of kin.

So which will you reach for?
The pink toes or the claws?
The lullaby or the war cry?
Either way, understand:
She's more than curled toes,
more than pretty dresses.
She is savage.

And every time you touch a page
you're brushing fingers
against the bars of her cage.

"The Ear"

Asking someone,
Can I talk to you?
Will you hear me?
Can I have your ear?

In between those lines—
if you're lucky—
the right kind of listener
will feel the fear,
hear the spiral
in the words you don't say,
the pauses that bend,
the breath that gives way.

The kind of ear
that lets you bleed—
unmeasured,
unguarded,
no tally, no need.

Where tears can fall
without want,
without pretense,
just truth arriving
without a sentence.

An ear where you're held,
seen,
met exactly where you are.
Not minimized.
Not asked to be small.
Not told who you should've been so far.

The kind where life is spoken
not in pretty words,
not dressed for applause,
but said in the raw—
the kind of truth
that can bruise before it heals,
that stings,
then steadies,

then teaches you what's real.

No posturing.
No bravado.
No need to perform or prove.

Just honesty
calling you
out of yourself
and back into you.

The kind of ear
that makes you stand taller,
shoulders square,
spine remembering how to rise.
The kind with a voice
that shakes the fear loose
and names the strength
you've tried to disguise.

Affirmations
that land right here

in the in-between,
where doubt and lies compete,
where truth needs somewhere
warm to take a seat.

Knowing you've been seen.
Knowing you've been heard.
Held
in the only way
that ever mattered.

It's not romantic.
It's not wild.

It's like being found.
Like being given breath—
breathed into—
not to save you,
just to remind you
you're still alive too.

Like watering dead earth
without promise or plan,
for no other reason
than believing it can.

No reasoning beyond the need.

It knows when you don't need answers,
just space
to bleed.

That kind of ear
doesn't wait
for the sound—
the crumble,
the spiral,
the breaking down.

It keeps space
before the fall,
for the fear,
for the call.

Open.
Brutally honest.
Steady.
Still.

That's the ear.
That's the need.

The space that whispers strength
when your voice can't speak.

The kind that makes standing here
even plausible.

An ear that makes me believe
this—
this night—
was possible.

"Pink Toes and Pretty Dresses"

Pouring words into these pages.

This is the safest avenue for that side of me.

Because unleashed, she's a beast—beautiful, yet free.
In her, you won't see me,

Not the version you brandish as graceful, heaven-sent.

She'll have you wrecked and bent.
Leave her in these pages—you're safer that way, son.
Stay away from the sun, don't fly too close,
she's just out of reach; you're not equipped to deal with the real me.

The smoke on my tongue,

Talons ready to shred you, wreck you.
I keep her in these pages—you don't know what she can do.

Nah, kid, this ain't for you.
She didn't come to make love; she's out for blood.

More than curled toes,
to her, you're a baby gazelle with your throat exposed

Nah, friend, she'll have you contacting your next of kin.
Leave her in these pages and protect your peace—
You'll come back in pieces.

Nah, dog, let this one pass you by.
Slide to the left, let it be,
because you do not know the real me.
The things I'm capable of.

Savage me.

You want docile and demure—
Pink toes, pretty dresses?
Depends on the me you get.

"The Collective"

I was the strong one—
the one who multiplied your shine.
The cheerleader, the coach,
late-night pep talks,
the *how was your day?*
the *if you need me, I'm on my way.*

A warm smile,
a steady shoulder,
a hand to wipe the tears away.

But when it came time for you to shine for me,
I got excuses and cloudy days.
No phone calls,
no hand at my back
where your warmth should have been.
The reasons for no-shows
got real old.

In my moments of high,
I searched the crowd for you—
for the support, the echo,
the same light I once poured into you.
No likes. No shares.
No *you got this, girl.*
Just silence,
and the hollow hum
of a one-sided love.

No breeze from my fan club,
no winds beneath my wings.
But still—
I flew.
I soared.

Heart heavy, but ready for flight.
My light dimmed but not gone.
No expectations now,
no need for reciprocation.

I won't dim my flame
to make yours burn brighter.
The emptiness will shift;
the burn will settle.

My destination remains unchanged—
no pause, no stop.
Just me,
moving through the silence,
rising through the quiet.

Because the collective of you
was never the collection I needed.
Those who throw *bestie* like confetti
disappear when it's my celebration.

Don't mistake these words for bitterness.
No—this is clarity.
Now I can just read the weather.

I'm still on my way up…
I just hoped we'd arrive together.

"Burn Bridges"

They say you can't just show up,
burn bridges, and call it self-care.

Baby, let me explain something —
I. Will. Angela Bassett that bitch.
(If you know, you know.)

I burn so I never go back.
Not out of spite — to preserve me.
To bar you from my mind, from my heart,
from the new me I'm building.

I scorch the path you once walked
so your footprints cannot lead me backward.
Ash on my hands, sure —
but no returning roads.
No backdoor keys.
No quiet undoing.

This is protection in flame:
I will burn everything to the ground
rather than hand you access to who I'm becoming now.

Not cruel. Not petty. Necessary.
My borders are a bonfire now —
warmth for me, warning for

I'll sip my cognac, watch the sparks,
and name it what it is: survival.
No room here for fakeness,
only the honest ruin that makes room for real.

So yes — watch the embers, learn the lesson:
I choose myself.
I guard my becoming.

I burn, and I rise.

"Not Playing Hard to Get"

A man I don't want swears I'm playing hard to get,
as if disinterest is some kind of performance,
as if my silence is an invitation.

He forgets—

I had one encounter that told me everything I needed to know. It wasn't
chemistry.

It was confirmation.

My "no" offends you,
like I owe you softness for showing up with a smile.
Like my worth is measured by how quickly I melt
when you call me "beautiful."

To another, you said I'm playing games.
So I looked it up—
to pretend to want what you don't,
to feign disinterest to make him chase.
But baby, there's no pretense here.
I'm not chasing,
not teasing

not withholding. I'm uninterested.

Your access is denied
not from pride,
but from discernment.

You lack that quiet kind of confidence,
the kind that doesn't need a woman's attention to feel alive.
You mistake pursuit for power,
lust for connection, and persistence for proof that you're worth wanting.

Every conversation circled back to sheets and skin,
to rooms with locked doors and dim lights.
Every call—an echo of ego.
Every knock—a test I stopped answering.

See, I've learned to listen
to what a man reveals when he thinks he's charming.
You said, "I can teach you pleasure."
But pleasure without understanding is empty.
You never studied the language of patience,
of subtlety, of presence.

Read *Dating for Dummies* if you must,
but no book can teach what your spirit lacks.

This isn't me playing hard to get.
This is me walking away from what doesn't feed me.

You call it a game. I call it growth.

Because the truth is,
you're not the kind of man who makes a woman stay—
you're the kind who reminds her
why she never should have come in the first place.

"Silver Lining, Spent Shell"

A silver lining, a spent shell.

a bullet dodged, a narrow hell.
Chaos like winter rain —
steps I'm blessed never to take again.

You looked like danger
in tan work boots,
smooth trigger disguised as a man,
eyes the color of gunmetal,
bound tighter than a hammer's spring.

I almost let you pull me under,
almost signed my name
in powder and flame.
But alarms live in the air,
the scent of smoke before the bang.
Something whispered,
step sideways,
and I did.

Thinking how close your bullet came
to threading through my life —
no powder burns in my skin,
no shrapnel in my heart.
Just the echo of danger,

lessons carved in the dark,
and the quiet relief of a clean escape.

"Burn"

I burn
not in destruction,
but in refinement.

To burn away the layers,
to see who I am
when the smoke clears.

Who I am is fluid now—
who I am,
who I was,
who I'll become.

You're used to head bowed,
folded hands,
legs crossed,
sweetness on my tongue.

But pendulums swing.
And questions rise
about the woman I'm becoming.

Trauma's blade
demands reckoning.
Nobody is ready for her.

She's the blaze—
turning what doesn't serve
into ash.

Safer to leave her in the past.
Maybe the starved one too—
the one who learned to survive
on emotional starvation,

forced independence,
and intrusive thoughts on rotation.

Let's leave *her* in the shadows.
Another version I dare not choose—
faded,
but still part of the truth.

So I set fire
to the damaged versions:

the tired,
the lonely,
the hurt,
the sacrificed,
the broken,
the drowning,
the unseen,
the critical,
the careful,
the scared,
the version frozen by fear.

I burn.
Not in destruction.
But for refinement.

To see who I am
when the smoke clears.

Beautiful.
But refined.
By the fire.

"After the Dust Settles"

I'm about to burn everything to the ground
behind my heart
and see what — and who — is left
after the dust settles.

With intrusive thoughts
and whispers,
my heart wrestles.

No breath strong enough
to keep my wings lifted.
No voices of love gifted.

Feelings shifted,
not even thrifted —
second-hand guesses
of where others stand.

Clarity in distress,
slipping like sand.
On this edge,
matches in hand.

My tiredness
has found its sound.

Yeah…
me burning it all
to the ground.

Fireproof.
Still standing.
A smoking tongue.

I'm what's left
after the dust settles.

Sharpening my heart,
no fucks to give —

 soft only for those
who stood in the fire,

who were my live wire,
who caught the spark,

who didn't let me explode,
who watched my heart wrestle,

and were still standing
when the dust settled.

"Touch Starved"

Touch starved,
in more ways than one.

Like my heart
can't remember the sun.
Warmth on my skin
a distant memory —
the gold of sunlight
reduced to gray.

Everything dimmed,
skies clouded over,
no vibrance,
no glow.

Empty.
Unfulfilled.
Hollow.

Shallow puddles
where oceans used to be.
No depth.
No lines.

My mind blank,
heart still.

Touch starved…

not just of hands,
but of being held
in someone's meaning.

I don't crave contact —
I crave connection.

Skin can be touched
without being felt.

I miss warmth
that didn't ask for anything in return.
I miss sunlight
that didn't leave bruises on my hope.

Skin remembers
what the heart tries to forget.

Touch starved...
not for bodies,
but for belonging.

"Cognac Cigar Nights and Black Coffee Mornings"

Cognac… cigar nights.
Black coffee… mornings.
The scent of your cigar
still ghosting my sheets.
The taste of your drink
lingering on my tongue.

I fought the battle—
yeah…
you won.

Remnants of our night
strewn in a pile on the floor,
breakfast bare,
black coffee
while still tangled in my sheets.

Whispered promises—
urges not to forget—
still tingle
at the nape of my neck.

My skin remembers
your kisses.
My limbs,
outstretched to your touch.
My hips remember your fingertips
and the heat
where my back dips.

I can still taste
the cognac from your lips.

So no—
I won't forget
how you traced my body
like you created it
out of time itself.

Poured into me
like you'd never
be anywhere else,
relishing every moment
in beautifully scented dreams
spun from cognac,
cigar nights,
and black coffee mornings.

"What Am I Doing Here"

What am I doing here
if you can't do
what life was breathed into you to do?

I was carved from you—
meant to be protected by you.
That includes my peace,
and these broken pieces.

Your chest should be my safe place,
carved and shaped
to fit my face.
A place to lay my fears,
designed to catch my tears.

This is DNA-coded.
This is instinct.
This is what you were created to do—
why life was breathed into you.

My spirit should ease when you are near.
If I am not your rib,
What am I doing here?

If life was breathed into you,
speak that life into me.
In your presence,
there should be nothing I fear.

Either you are the lion before me—
or tell me
What am I doing here?

In my moments of weakness,
you should be my strength.
When I am broken.
When I am bent.

You were meant to be a lover.
A refuge.
A friend.

You were meant to be a shelter,
not a storm I survive.

A place where my breath slows,
not where I learn to brace.

If I have to shrink to be kept,
this isn't love — it's labor.

If my softness is a liability,
you are not my home.

I won't beg for safety
from the one built to give it.

If I'm not your rib — then ask yourself…

What are *you* doing here.

HEAT

"Chapter 2 — Where I Begin"

In chapter two — where I begin,
trust,
you don't want this smoke, friend.

Chapter one gave you soft,
quiet,
head bowed,
a plain.

Chapter two erupts
with a new voice,
fire and flame.

Stop at the door
and assess the room,
'cause you'll find
a new voice in bloom.

Don't expect the quiet,
the shy,
the demure.

I'm screaming my truth
and I **will** ask
what you came for.

Reciprocation on demand now
for the way I pour.

Meeting your gaze —
Unflinching.
Unphased.

Legs crossed,
back straight,
smoke on these lips,
no remorse on my tongue.

No battles left to be had.
I **won**.

Approach with respect.
Approach with intent.

This chapter is where I begin.

And this new smoke?

Is. Not. What. You. Want. Friend.

"I Belong To Me"

Tonight, I belong to me.
Phone face down, door locked,
curtains drawn while I wipe away
makeup and remnants of the day.

Taking off all the hats—
Sister. Wife. Lover. Friend. Caregiver.
All the women in me are tired.

Water rising in the tub
like a molten whisper,
steam curling up my thighs
while music coils the air.
I slide under,
skin surrendering to oils and heat,
stress unbuttoned,
each sigh a weighted release.

Fingers trace my own skin,
slow maps of every chore,
every to-do list,
every need of someone else—
leading nowhere but back to me.

The drink burns,
my pulse answers.
Tension dissolves over steam,
water spilling,
time bending.

My glass tilts,
and I don't care.

Tonight I belong to me—
glass empty,
steam a ghost on the mirror.

I watch my reflection
and smile:
this was mine to give,
mine to take,
mine to savor—
my time still humming
under my skin.

Tomorrow
I'll pick up the hats again.

"Patio Nights"

Patio nights—jazz music and vodka flights.
Men dressed to the nines,
women gliding finer than wine.

Before I even hit the door
I can feel you there—
a tension in my spine,
your scent riding the night air.

It skipped across the wind
and found me at the car—
that unmistakable trace
of that Churchill cigar.

Aroma strong enough
to make Winston proud,
seductive enough
to part the crowd.

I find your smile as your eyes catch mine,
smoke slipping past your lips
and slowing time.

That slow grin,
that tilt of your head—
says you're glad to see me;
I take my time instead.

Across the room you draw in
that sultry smoke—
I'm instantly envious
of the Churchill between your lips,
fighting off thoughts
of those lips,

your tongue,
your hands on my hips.

Me on tiptoe,
tasting the last drop
of your cognac kiss.

"I Drink"

I used to drink.

To forget, to close the door.
To mask feelings I didn't know how to hold.
To numb myself into choices I now cringe to recall.
To turn nightmares into distant, blurred memories.
To chase sleep that swallowed me whole, silent and deep.

Now, I drink
As an adult, aware, savoring each sip
Something strong, something sweet, at the end of the day
A glass over dinner, the clink of crystal soft against the table
A glass with a lover, a friend, laughter curling around us
Brandy in a bath, steam rising, the world melting away
Velvet warmth pooling in my hands, my chest, my thoughts

I pour slowly
Amber light spilling into crystal

Warmth curling over me, settling into mind and body
A taste of sweetness, a burn of fire
I sip alone, or with lips pressed close
Nothing to hide, nothing to chase

No guilt
No shame
Just presence
Just pleasure
Just power
Just me

Every sip a reclamation
Every glass a kiss from myself to myself
A slow, deliberate savor

A knowing smile
A quiet triumph

"Loved by the Storm"

Your storm came
and lifted me off my foundation.
Thunder cracked.
Lightning struck.
Ugly words — then kisses,
on rotation.

Never knew

when the clouds would go gray,
which words were soft enough to say.
I learned to manage
the changes
in the weather of the day.

Your voice, loud —
but your hands
found my softness,
strength followed by caress,

confusion dressed as tenderness.

Your storms weakened
a foundation built on sand.
A love language
that sounded more like a command.

Learning not to flinch
at your touch.
Reading your moods
like the weather,
bracing for the foundation to be rocked.
Learning to be loved by the storm —

caressed by hurricane winds,
walking in love's floodwaters.

Wanting to drown,
but learning to swim.

Bracing for rage's downpour,
leaning into the wind,
discovering how to bend
but not break.

Loving in the storm.
Learning to love the storm.

While being
loved
by the storm.

"How Are You"

You asked how are you
Noticing pains shadow in my midst.

This.

This is what men do.
What *you* do..

You can see in my face
the wreckage that was my day.

Me being off-kiltered
makes you real unfiltered.

Your breath in your chest —
I see the change in you.
That switch
that makes you do what men do.

Stepping into my space,
whispering how are you.

The space between my shoulder and my neck —
that's where your breath rests
as you ask again, how are you.

I'm fine, I reply.

At my hips your hands grip
as you kiss the lie from my lips,
whispering I'm not one of your little friends.
Don't lie to me again

Love…

I asked how are you.
This is what men do.
What *you* do.

The heat in your voice.
That tone. That intimacy.
A truth travels through me.

You step back.
I lean in.

You search my face,
making sure I'm steady,
that I can breathe again.

You let me spill the day's fears.
Your thumb wipes away my tears.

You hold the space
till my thoughts are stable,
keeping my gaze,
not rushing me till I'm able.

Your hand rests at my waist,
waiting for words I can't say.
Your touch melts away
the roughness of the day.

Your chest tight
till the words I'm okay —
said not the way I quote to

'my little friends'
but the way that lets *you* breathe again.

To know I've fallen back into me,
in a way you believe,
a way you can see.

The only way you trust that it's true —
is in your embrace
I finally melt into you.

Settling into ease,
stepping into me,
moving into my space.

Between my shoulder and my neck
you place your face —
your favorite place
to rest your breath.

You're content
that my need was met.

You whisper
this is what you'll always do.
When the days get hard —
find you.

You step back,
taking my hand,
running your thumb
across my wedding band.

You murmur low,
you're good.
You can stand.

Now I need you to go home
to your man.

I did what you needed me to do.
Please —
you're reminding me
that I'm still a man too.

"Chapter Two Energy"

For years now, the word *change* sat heavy on my chest,
giving birth to what I call Chapter Two at its best.
The kind of energy that burns it all down,
where truth survives flames and pretenders don't stick around.

In the fire lives this me — unfiltered, untamed,
the real one rising, no longer contained.
The one you won't survive... or maybe you might,
depends if you're fireproof, built for this light.

This isn't destruction, it's careful design,
refinement through burning, shedding old time.
Your notions of me curl up in smoke,
the pedestal crumbles, the cage finally broke.

Sweet.
Demure.
Heaven-sent grace.
Those labels dissolve, can't keep up with my pace.
Legs crossed, head bowed, hands folded just right,
that version was safe — acceptable, light.

Comfortable. Managed. Easy to hold.
A story you liked, predictable, old.
But the fire is starting, a bonfire at last,
setting flame to the versions I outgrew fast.

Dust and ash are all that remain,
smoke resting heavy on my tongue like a name.
My pages lie blank, but my ink tells the truth,
bleeding new language, unburdened, uncouth.

The woman in these flames — you may not survive her,
she's sharper, she's braver, she's no longer quieter.

Change settles in deep, no longer a plea,
it's rooted, it's solid — the realest of me.

Still burning.

Still learning.
Still shedding what's old.
Still Chapter Two energy — fearless and bold.

"A Change (Part 2)"

For a few years now
the word *change* has sat heavy on me.

Giving birth to what I call
Chapter Two energy—
the kind that burns everything to the ground.

In the flames lives this me.
The real me.

The one you won't survive.
Or you might.

Are you fireproof?

This isn't destruction.
This is refinement.

Shedding your preconceived notions of me.
Burning the pedestal you placed me on.
Turning your caging terms to ash—
sweet,
demure,
heaven-sent,
graceful.

Legs crossed.
Head bowed.
Folded hands.

That version was acceptable.
Safe.
Managed.
Comfortable.

But the fire is starting now.
A bonfire.

Dust and ash are what's left of her.
Smoke sits on my tongue.

My pages are blank.
My ink bleeds a new truth.

The woman in this flame—
you may not survive her.

Change is settling
into the real me.

Still…
Chapter Two energy.

"In the After"

In the After
in the quiet spaces,
when lips have left my skin,
when my hands are free of you—

that space where my heart is still,
still waiting,
needing.

What's not found in breath,
not found in
limbs,
sweat,
heat, and skin—

What's left to meet that need.

This is where your heart should meet me.
Pour into me ideas of real intimacy,
where my mind is fed beyond our bed.
Presence with truth—
just every inch of you.

Conquering my body, you've proved to be easy.
Challenge—conquer the rest of me:
my ideas, thoughts, my curiosity.

Show me you can handle me,
all of me—
the parts that are in the aftermath
of love's races.

Meet the need
in those quiet spaces.

Can you—
meet that part of me, too.

Will you feed more than my body,
let your breath entice my mind?
A world you've never known
is what you'll find.

My existence is yours at will,
living in the quiet spaces
where my heart stills.

"Threshold"

I am at a threshold of who I am.
Who I'm becoming.

The destination is set.
Stagnation in—I haven't stepped through that door yet.

Mental bags are packed.
Against myself, negative thoughts are stacked.

Becoming waits on the other side.
Destination memorized.
My heart knows the route.

But I haven't stepped through.
Still standing in my fear.
Weaponizing my own voice against myself.

This threshold.
Bags packed mentally.
No movement.

Becoming presses its forehead against the glass.
Arguing with myself as fear whispers lies.
Calls my stagnation, preparation.
Patience.
Says it's anything but fear.

The noise gets louder
as success feels near.

I recognize the lies
by how familiar they sound.

The door doesn't move.
I do.

"Let Me Drown"

They watched me drown,
Still handed me bricks
To build a walkway
So their feet would never get wet.

Said things like,
Be glad you've got a pool to drown in —
You get the water for free.
Their bridges built
From standing on me.

Bent.
Broken.
Tired.
But no one sees.

I set myself on fire
to warm them a few degrees.
No hand lifted to keep me above water,
still slipping under,
spilling fluid from my lungs
Just to keep them watered —
To make sure they grow,
that their dreams come true.

You'd think they'd turn,
see me —
See I'm losing my strength.
Each time I come up for air,
it takes longer.
Still, they never stop reaching for their goals,
never toss a line.

I keep holding up their boat,
Smiling.
Dare not frown.
Everything's fine —
Tow the line.

All the while thinking,
maybe it's better to drown.
To let them get wet.
To stop saving others
with my last breath.

To finally let my tiredness have a sound.
To reclaim myself
from those
Who let me drown.

SKIN

"Long Days"

The week has been long,
and my day longer.

Craving something liquid and dark—
darker than these thoughts.

Patience?

I have less.

Tired?

Yes.

Adulthood took the rest.

Exhausted at the seams.
Music therapy
in need.

First sip burns,
and the hours won't stop.

And then...
that beat drops.
Slow and steady.

My pulse slows.
My breath catches,
pulling down thoughts,
memories.

Images of smoke,
heat,
and skin.

Tip of your tongue tracing my neck.
Hands on these hips.
Your heat where my back dips.

Letting you taste
The heat of my day.

Those hands
finding my need.
Fingertips
searching for my release.

All of you
Dipping into me.

Your fire.
This steam.
Our rhythm.
The flame.

Skin and heat—
moans of my name.

The air is thick
as our melanin drips.

In the rocking,
the gripping,
my pulse trips.

These eyes—
closed.

My breath—
held.

Your body—
shaking.

Our release—
found.

Pleasure murmurs
in satisfaction's sound.

"The First Time"

Pulling down memories of the first time.

And the words still escape my lips.

Yet, years later the heat from your

fingertips still rest on my hips.

The heat from your tongue at the back of my legs.

The taste of your tongue.

The sweat on your skin.

You took your time.

Unaware you were the first.

Your hands pulled down insecurities.

Mending things you didn't break.

Whispering my name in that quiet room.

Touching parts of me I didn't know existed.

Leaving a trail that's lasted a lifetime.

Indelibly imprinted in the first time.

"My Exhale"

Catching the scent of wine on your breath
as our rhythm parts the veil.
Your face reveals the satisfaction
in the dip of my hips with every exhale.

Eyes closed, your breath caught in your chest,
head tilted back, your body blessed.
Still closed eyes—
your waist made to fit the curve of my thighs.
Hands trace my shoulders—
a path you don't need light to see,
pulling me down,
you rising to meet me.

Bare chests, sweat and melanin,
simmering together like game prizes—
and we both win.
The smoke between us
has to be a sin.

Heat brings water droplets
traveling between my breasts.
You trace them
until they find their eternal rest,
just shy of my navel,
where your fingers now reside,
searching for the lost ones
that slipped inside.

Eyes shift once you find
more than you were looking for.
Dripping lines.
Fixed eyes in mine.
Fingers working like you're picking a lock,

looking for the prize—
humb on the dial,
relishing my cries.

Your wine-scented tongue
where my shoulder meets my neck.
Enjoying letting you
do only what you can do.
I meet your smile
as my hips dip to greet you.

My breath caught in my chest
as we reach the end of our tale—
the evidence of your satisfaction
drips in
my
Exhale.

"Slow Burn"

The smoke slipping from your lips,
the taste of whisky on your tongue,
the scent of your cigar
lingering in a slow burn.

The look in your eyes,
the promise in the air—
whispering it'll soon be my turn.

My body will replace the smoke on your lips,
the bend of my neck
a new home for your tongue.

Let the cigar burn,
scents filling the air
for ecstasy's terms.
Let the smoke curl around your fingertips,
tracing the place where my back dips.
Give your whisky-laced lips
a taste of my tongue.

The growl in your chest
tells me I've already won.

Fulfill the promises your eyes made
earlier,
when you watched me
over the flame.

Whispering over your glass
the rules to this game,
wanting, asking, begging
for me to wait my turn.

you watch as tension builds,
reveling
in my slow burn.

"Hey You"

Two little words.
Mixed with that tone you only get with me—

Warm. Settling. Intimate.

My days instantly better,
my heart beats different.

Hey you.
My love.
My friend.
My past and present.

Hey you.
A mischievous grin.
lips that leave traces of heat.
Fingertips that still ache to reach for me.

Hey you.
How was your day?
Loves in your look,
not what you say.

Hey you.
Still has the power to unsettle me.

Hey You.
Still makes my heart skip.

Hey you.
Will always belong to me.

That drop in tone,
synonymous with my name.

Hey you.
Comes from a love tamed.
Tamed into comfort,
settled into familiarity.

Hey you,
in that tone reserved just for me

Dangerously warm.
Dangerously settling.
Dangerously intimate.

Still makes my heart beat different.

"Unhinged"

You asked about my look.
It says don't play with me.

It's unmasking my need,
unearthing unhinged sides of me.

In just a moment,
I promise you'll get it.
Don't play with it.
I need you to stand up in it.

Bring that grown folks energy.

Whispers of the things you'll do,
moaned into my neck,
I need you to undo me —
emotionally,
physically,
metabolically.

Grip these hips.
Pull me into you.
Your breath at my lips,
promising all of you —
every inch,
every moan.

Head tilts.
My body groans.
My breath gone.
Too late to run.
Body already undone.

Mind tipping at ecstasy's edge,
sanity and breath
still gripping the bed.
Only word escaping me is *please*.

Your rhythm building something in me,
hidden behind a scream
shuddering free.

Air thick
with that grown folks energy.

"Wicked Smile"

I watch you sleep,
and something wickedly feminine
rests in the curve of my smile.

Dragging my hands across your chest,
my breath catches —
I wait,
refusing to breathe
until I hear it…

that slow, deep growl
that escapes you,
even in sleep,
at my touch.

You reach for me mindlessly,
pulling me into you,
fingertips tracing my spine,
your breath heavy in the room.

And the moment I realize
it's mine,
I place a kiss on your neck
and the growl gets deeper —

your breath
sleep-induced,
ragged.

In the dark, without hesitation,
without consciousness or thought,

your body chooses me
before your mind does.

You feel me
before you see me.
You hold me
like instinct.

Not reason.
Not thought.

Just truth.

My wicked smile waits for you.
Even in sleep you search for me—
instinct taking over,
hands on my hips,
breath on my neck.

Your growl is mine.
Heat growing at the base of my spine.
Awakening to my wicked smile.

Now give me what's mine.

With Gratitude

Thank you for reading *Cognac Kisses.*
For letting these pages touch you.
For leaning into the smoke, the heat, the skin—and the quiet that lingers after.

This book lives in spaces where desire meets honesty.
Where wanting isn't rushed.
Where intimacy isn't only what happens in the dark, but what remains when the bodies separate and the truth stays.

If something here awakened you, unsettled you, softened you, or reminded you of yourself—then we shared the moment exactly as intended.

Your thoughts, reflections, and reviews are always welcome.

Find me at
https://jmariepublishing.com/diana-williams-kirklin-1

www.ingramcontent.com/pod-product-compliance
Lightning Source LLC
Chambersburg PA
CBHW071441300726
48976CB00004B/1409